"Dear Magnificent Being,

When you Love yourself unconditionally

You inspire others to Love themselves unconditionally

When you Love yourself unconditionally

You think, act and speak in ways that create more Love around you

When you Love yourself unconditionally

You raise the vibration of the collective consciousness

When you Love yourself unconditionally

You honour yourself and all life

When you Love yourself unconditionally

You are uplifting and empowering all life on Mother Earth"

-unknown

Falling for the girl in the mirror

Chapter 1

Self- love. The word says it all. Self-love is the regard for one's own happiness or advantage influenced by an individual's idea of the world, self-esteem, and beliefs of what is right and wrong. Self-love can be an extremely tricky skill to acquire in today's time. We live in a world where the word "selfish "or the phrase "full of themselves "gets exchange routinely as if it were money, an object glorified and viewed as necessary and scarce. A world where we often get criticized for embracing our remarkable bodies and it leads us to trust that self-love is wrong. Why should you endure feeling awful for purely being you? Why is it so hard to tell that breath-taking creation in the mirror that every edge and mark on their body is fascinating? Where did it all start?

As children, we are raised to regard that the sky is the limit and that we can be whatever we want to be. Babies operate on a scheme where they are taught what is right or wrong as they cannot quite analyse situations just yet as their brains are still developing. Our brains were created in such a way where we learn and design our lives by interpreting and adapting to the world.

Our actions are supported by habits and habits are supported by memory which is created through experiences. A simple example of this can be fashion. If I purchase an orange garment and people react in a praising manner to me wearing orange, the chances of me purchasing orange clothing are higher, as opposed to me wearing a green dress and people reacting in a pessimistic manner making it less prone for me to purchase green clothing. We feed off and react based on the energy given to us. The same notion can be applied to body image.

At age six most of us would run around in shorts and take swims wearing nothing but underwear and nevertheless feel great about ourselves. As time progresses and you approach your pre-teen years where puberty becomes a huge part of your lives and hormonal imbalances occur leading to drastic emotional and physical changes.

In some cases, you look around and notice that you might be the only one changing. This is where things tend to get a little dark. You look around and you notice people laughing at you and in most cases, people start to bully you. Suddenly the world becomes dark and eating disorders might start to creep up on you and depression starts to become less of a word and more of a constant reminder that you are not good enough and your brain starts to become your own worst enemy. What started as home for happy memories turns into a host for dark thoughts.

Chapter 2

My story

I would say I had a quite decent childhood. I grew up in a loving home with both parents and I was encouraged to dream big. Every other Sunday afternoon we would share a meal prepared by my wonderful mother and caring aunt. My dad would always ask me the same question in the same casual tone," Gloria, what do you want to be when you grow up?" with hopes of me responding in an energetic scream "A Doctor!" but unfortunately, he got a different and unexpected answer each time. Some days I would respond by saying "an astronaut "or "Mr. Bean "or even a nurse. I truly believed I could achieve all these great things.

Come grade six and he would ask me the same question and this time I would respond with things more down to earth like "an actor "or "businesswomen ". The only difference between the six-year-old Gloria's response and the twelve-year-old Gloria's response is the self-confidence in her answers. Society had altered me and robbed me of my dreams and aspirations just so that I could fit in and "belong somewhere". I was taught to conform to someone else's expectations of me and my future just so that they would not feel insecure about themselves or threatened. Dream big slowly turned into Be realistic, my opinion into your opinion and goals turned into a waste of time. Now that's where I went wrong. The biggest mistake ever. Settling for mediocracy.

I was living in a world where everything was changing, everything including me. I had traded my confidence and gut instinct for acceptance. I had to change so much that the alteration process eventually caused damage. I was broken. I was taught to be a modest young lady who kept quiet, never questioned anything and to view the world in a certain way.

I grew up with an older sister who was viewed as the goal and person you should strive to be. She had the top grades, she participated in almost all the school's events, she was quiet, and she had an amazing body. My measurement of success was according to how similar I was to my sister. I was reminded to be like her, act like her and mimic her every move. Which led me to let go of my identity but ironically, I would always somehow get my identity back in possession when she was around.

My sister and I were extremely close. I felt like she understood me and saw me as me and not a duplicate version of herself. She would never comment on my weight and whenever I was with her, I felt safe and confident, I felt like me. Sadly, all good things end. She had matriculated and was going to move away to attend university. I was devastated.

Chapter 3

The crisis

I cried myself to sleep and every morning the sound of birds chirping would interrupt my dreams and I would awaken to what I then viewed as a harsh reality(things are never that bad, you just need to look around and surely you will find beauty from pain). My pillar of strength was gone. The teasing began and I did not feel safe nor comfortable talking to adults about my emotions and struggles as most of the harsh comments were coming from them. Unfortunately for me, I believed their sharp words. I turned to food for support and that is when I started to gain weight. What had happened is simply an example of the Law of Attraction and sub-conscious manifestation. I was constantly told that I was overweight and I constantly told myself that I was overweight. My negative self-talk and my words soon turned into reality.

I stopped taking care of myself but of course, Gloria being Gloria, I covered my bad habits with a fake simile and an occasional "I'm fine' when I was not fine. My world once painted in bright joyful colours turned black and white. At that time, I connoted the word "fat" with feelings of disgust and unpleasantness

I had finally done it. I had hit rock bottom. My sweet precious tears were running down my cheeks like a powerful stream of water destroying everything in its path. "Do it, do it "I heard a voice say but then I caught a glimpse of myself in the mirror as I sat on the cold white bathroom floor. I could not believe what I saw. A beautiful soul who had let the world mould her into what they viewed as acceptable and of course, there were so many versions of what was acceptable. I could not help but think about my dear sister and what she would say if she saw me like this. I slowly walked towards the mirror and looked at the Goddess in the mirror through my teary eyes. What had I become? I wiped my tears with my wet jersey and for some odd reason, I recited the lines from a movie I watched: "You are kind. You are smart. You are beautiful ". Of course, I did not believe those words, but it kept me stable. The year ended and the next year unfolded. I decided to participate in school plays because it would allow me not to be me for a few minutes. Those few minutes were enough to gradually restore myself to a better me.

That day at the bathroom was the end. It was the end of the girl who would believe everything someone told her, the girl who would settle for anything other than what she deserved. That day was the end of that girl and the birth of a fearful young lady who would bring joy into people's lives. It was not easy, but it just shows how a simple sentence can be life-changing and how great things are always around and how you just need to look in the right places. I lived for the stage. I lived for my family and the bright smile my friends would put on my face and vice versa. I lived for moments with my teachers. I lived for me and that was honestly one of the best decisions of my life.

Chapter 4

Aftermath

Let me keep it real with you. It was defiantly not easy. Times would be hard, and clouds would be dark. Days where I thought that it would be easier to give up and motivational quotes would not do justice, but faith kept me going.

I did not morph into the person I am today overnight, I took it one step at a time. I would smile to myself every time I walked past the mirror and eventually my self- esteem levels elevated, and my confidence levels increased over time. One repeated action eventually created a habit that turned into a life-long belief. My one advice for anybody going through the recovery phase would be to go easy on themselves and remember that lasting results take a prolonged period enriched with optimism and consistency. I promise that eventually, you WILL BE OKAY. If you are spiritual or religious that I encourage you to use that to your advantage by trusting in powers greater than you. Surely you were not created and this higher being just decided to leave you to struggle alone

Chapter 5

The Law Of Attraction

Honestly, if I knew about the "The Secret " during my days of trials and tribulations everything else would have been so much easier and faster so I want to give you an introduction and exposure to the Law of Attraction and I encourage you to look more into it and start consciously applying it to your life.

Let us start with a definition. According to Successonious.com; It is the attractive magnetic power of the Universe that draws similar energies together and manifests it through the power of creation hence the following points relate and are true about the Law of Attraction:

1. What you give in you is what you get out.

2. It is one of the 12 Universal Laws that uphold the universe therefore it is always working regardless of your belief in it and it is currently happening right now in your life as we speak. Saying that the Law of Attraction is not working for you is equivalent to saying that gravity is not working for you.

3. You create your reality, you make your life want you want it to be.

4. Thoughts turn into ideas, ideas turn into beliefs, beliefs turn into manifestations and manifestation create reality.

5. You manifest on 3 levels: conscious, sub-conscious and unconscious (also known as the energetic level).

6. EVERYTHING is energy and energy is everything.

7. You are responsible for everything in your life.

Point 1: What you give in you is what you get out

I am sure that you are all familiar with the biblical expression "what you sow you shall reap". Manifestation is all about mindset. I cannot emphasize how important mindset is! The human mind has powers beyond imagination and is responsible for phenomenal occurrences that not even scientists can explain. If you have a negative and fixed mindset then your reality will be filled with undesirable events but if you have a growth and positive mindset and you see things when possible in a white light, then your goals will be achievable, and your reality will be desirable.

We all have the same 24 hours. What separates you from your role model is your mindset and your inspired action. How you spend your 24 hours. Your inspired action is what activates your desired manifestation. The recipe for manifestation is thought+ inspired action +

intention(emotion). The designated formula specific to self-love is hope/faith+ affirmations/mediations/acts of kindness + love = unconditional self-love.

*Note that the strongest vibration (energy level) is love *

The time it takes to manifest self-love into your reality and the time it takes to reach the desired self-esteem level will differ from person to person because you need to be ready to receive your manifestation. Think of it as you having a cup filled with impure water to the rim and you wanting fresh clean drinking water in the same cup, you would need to empty your cup before pouring in the new water. You need to empty your vessel to receive (how you empty your cup will differ from person to person as your cup way be filled with different things e.g. some people empty their cup by forgiving themselves or accepting their reality .)

Point 2: The Law of Attraction is one of the 12 universal laws and It works regardless of your belief in it.

You are constantly living your life by the Law Of Attraction whether it is on a unconscious level or sub-conscious level. An example of the manifestation formula applied is being hungry: hunger + getting food + hopeful to be satisfied = full stomach.

Another example of the energies at work is how if you enter a room filled with irritable people and you engage with those people, you will eventually become irritable and anyone else that enters the room is most likely to feel that same emotion or mood. The key is to use the Law of Attraction to your advantage. For example, wanting to earn a higher income: the want to be wealthy + trusting in the universe (set it and forget it) or even asking for a promotion + prosperity = larger income. You can literarily apply this formula to any goal.

The thought serves as notification to the universe to say that you are wanting to receive what you want to attract, the inspired action brings whatever you desire into the physical reality, you must remember that energy is everything although it is not visible in its simplest form to the physical world however it exists on a universal level just like atoms and electricity and whatever you are trying to manifest already exists although we cannot always see in our physical reality and lastly the most important component, emotion.

Emotion is energy in motion hence the name and we must understand that energy is always moving and changing its state (Law of conservation – energy cannot be created nor destroyed but transferred from one form to another) applying emotion allows for the conversion of what you are manifesting from an energetic state to a physical state. One thing to also remember when manifesting is that there is enough, we need to detach ourselves from the idea of scarcity and remember that there is enough money and love to go around

Point 3: You create your reality and you made your life want you want it to be

The law attraction allows you to create your reality through choices. Surely life could not have been all fate. If different materials of matter in different quantities were present during the Big Bang, there is a huge possibility that all this might not have occurred. Could it have been fate that the big bang occurred in such a way where earth was the only planet where life could exist in what was then perfection conditions? Could it fate your ancestors settled in a certain place at a specific time and age? Could it be fate that you are reading this exact book? I think not, so many things could have gone and there are just too many variables involved, one might even dare to say everything that has happened was carefully planned out.

Everything that is happening Is all part of a bigger whole or the bigger picture. You create your reality and you can also change it at any time. You are the author of your life. This is your story. This is your life. Your choices do not define you, but they most certainly do affect your future.

Point 4: Thoughts turn into ideas, ideas turn into beliefs, beliefs turn into manifestations and manifestation create reality.

Look around you. Everything originated from a thought. Take shoes as an example. someone saw the demand for shoes and thought of shoes as a solution. That person might have spread the idea or designed the shoe as an inspired action then finally might have felt excited about the project resulting in the production of the shoe. We can change our thoughts. Incorporate optimism into your daily life and one small repeated action eventually creates your reality.

Unfortunately, or fortunately for some people, not every single thought turns into reality. Your thought needs to be supported by action and it must be constant. It may seem impossible and overwhelming to change your beliefs that were installed in your sub-conscious mind from a young age but breaking the task up into small manageable pieces helps makes the process easier.

Point 5: You manifest on 3 levels: conscious, sub-conscious and unconscious/energetic

Conscious level- the state where you are aware of everything that is happening. Right now, you are conscious of the fact that The Law of Attraction exists. Most people manifest on this level as it is simple and practical. Manifestation on this level includes repeating affirmations and breath-work. I advise you to use this level first on your journey to self-love. Doing something as simple as taking deep breaths in and out while counting to ten during a time of conflict or even practicing mindfulness to calm you down can go a long way.

Sub-conscious -95 % of the things you do are on the sub-conscious level for example you don't tell your body to breathe and your heart to beat every second. Your body does it automatically through your sub-conscious mind and you are mostly unaware of it. Here is a question for you. What is your name? hopefully you know what the answer is. Your mind automatically found the answer to that question. Another example is your facial expressions. You did not tell your body to do it. manifesting in this state may be done by meditations during the beta state that extended into your sleep, calming music with positive words and surrounding yourself with positive vibes. In most cases your sub-conscious mind is your worst enemy when filled with unnecessary information and "re-wiring "your mind is necessary.

Re-wiring is the process of replacing bad habits with good habits for example deciding to stay off social media an hour before bed as this is the phase where you start to enter the beta brainwave state which is the state were you absorb the most information which is why most people study in the mornings and nights . In some cases you might be casually scrolling through Instagram and see someone who meets your levels of beauty and you might wish you were like them and you may carry this desire into your sleep and in the future, you might find yourself feeling insecure because you don't look like that person. Instead of going through your social media before bed and in the morning, do something productive like reading a book.

Unconscious/ Energetic: This is the level that people are not aware of. As humans, we set goals and make decisions based off information we are familiar with for example 5 years ago my goal would to be part of the top 10 because it existed and I knew people in it compared to me making the goal to finish writing this book because I did not know that I would be writing a book. On this level, you are unaware that a certain thing even exists. You don't know what your capabilities are, you don't know how much you can love yourself.

Point 6. EVERYTHING is energy and Energy is everything

Lets first break matter down to its basic components, atoms. Atoms are the building blocks of matter and matter is everywhere even the universe is made up of all kinds of matter like Plasma and dark matter. If you take anything, for example, a chair or leaf and you put it under an electron microscope, you will eventually you will see atoms and those atoms are energy as they are constantly moving. Once you understand this it will guide you on your path to understanding the universe. When you bring this up to a macroscopic level you will understand that you carry energy in different frequencies and vibrations and these always shifting as energy is always moving and transforming its form.

This is evident in nature. Where there is life, nothing is ever still. Once we understand that we all carry different frequencies at different times we can learn how to react better and more mature in certain situations of conflict for example if someone is teasing you or criticizing your body, you can identify that that person is experiencing a lower hateful frequency coming from a place of insecurity and from there you can help the person feel good about themselves and lift their vibration while uplifting your vibrations resulting in you feel good about yourself and in the end, both people have a high powerful vibration of love.

7. You are responsible for everything in your life
So far, we know that we are constantly

manifesting everything in our lives, and we create our future and we can change our beliefs, emotions, and intentions, right? This means that everything in our life from birth till death is because of us hence we are responsible for our reality. It is critical to start taking ownership for the things in our lives. You are born given tools like parents, siblings and from there you decide what you do with those tools. Think of it as a race, there are thousands of competitors participating in the same race. The winner is not determined by who reaches the finish the race first but by who makes the most out of their experience and who is most creative with the resources given. At the starting line, we are given certain resources. Some are given parents some are not, some are given money, and some are not. We choose what we do with the resources we are given or what we are not given. We are born in different environments and different levels of wealth and we choose how we create our life with those tools. You might have depression and from there life could go in so many ways. You could get anti-depressants and the side effects may change your life in either a positive or negative way or you could commit suicide (please don't) and it will affect your loved ones in ways beyond imagination or you could use the Law of Attraction which will change your life forever. You always have a choice in life and the outcome will be determined by what path you choose.

Chapter 7
Getting back in the game

I would like to treat self-love as a normal relationship and from my observance to have a lasting successful relationship takes a lot of work and commitment and from talking to different people, I gathered the communalities and a good relationship has the following main characteristics.

·   **<u>Acceptance</u> –** Accept yourself completely, yes may have had a terrible past that has changed your life but at some stage, you need to stop living in the past. You cannot change your past, but you can change your present and future. Your flaws are what make you beautiful. I may not know you on a personal level, but I cannot express how special you are. Yes, you! Repeat after me. I AM BEAUTIFUL INSIDE AND OUT AND MY PAST DOES NOT DEFINE ME!

·   **<u>Never give up-</u>** Never give up on yourself. The mountain seems too high until you start taking your first few steps and eventually you will be on the top. Always be willing to work on you. There will be days where people will turn a blind eye on your struggle and those are the days where you need to be there for you.

·   **Put in effort-** Every relationship regardless of the nature takes work. you need to be willing to want to love you. Take time to nurture your relationship with yourself. You are worth it.

·   **Expression of feelings-** It is already a lot that you might be hiding your true feelings from the world. There should be no need to pretend when you are with yourself. Accept your feelings. It is okay to feel guilty from time to time. Just remember that your emotions are powerful and remember that sub-conscious manifestation is always happening. Be honest with yourself and try to lift your mood when needed.

·   **Get to know your partner –** Take time to know yourself. You need to be okay with being alone in a room with no outside interaction. Get to know your likes and dislikes. If you know that you are a person who does not like conflict, then in future you will know not to put yourself in a situation where you will have to deal with conflict.

· **Love –** As I mentioned earlier on. Love is the highest and most powerful vibration. Invest in lots and lots of love into the relationship and like the Law of Attraction states, you will get love back.

· **Patience –** The chances of this all happening overnight are very slim, it is possible but unlikely. Good things take time. Take time for yourself and pamper yourself and most importantly you need to be obsessed with the process. It will need loads and loads of patience but of course, you can do it.

10-day self-love challenge

Day 1

"To love who you are, you cannot hate the experiences that shaped you "

- Andrea Dykstra

· Complete a meditation, these are available on YouTube or apps such as Headspace or Simple habit ☐

· Make a list of 52 POSTIVE things you love about yourself and put it in an area you will see every day ☐

· Drink 10 cups of water ☐

· Do something that makes you happy ☐

" Love yourself first and everything else will fall into line. You really have to love yourself to get anything done in this world "-Lucille Ball

Day 2

· Look at the list with the 52 things you love about yourself ☐

· Write a list of things you are grateful for. ☐

· Drink 10 glasses of water ☐

· Talk to a friend or family member about what
you are going through or just catch up with them. □

"Even if it makes others uncomfortable. I will love myself. "

-Janelle Monáe

Day 3

· Look at your 52-self-love list ☐

· Help someone ☐

· Clean your living space ☐

· Drink 10 glasses of water ☐

"The best way to be loved is to love yourself"

                       - Adam Lambert

Day 4

· Smile. ☐

· Make a dream board or list of where you wish to see yourself in 2 years ☐

· Drink 10 glasses of water ☐

· Look at the list ☐

"You are free. You are powerful. You are good. You are love. You have value. You have a purpose. All Is well ."- Abraham hicks

Day 5

· Make a new list with 48 more things you love about yourself ☐

· Drink 10 glasses of water ☐

· Spend the entire day without a cellular device or wi-fi ☐

· Take a relaxing warm bath or shower ☐

"Be your own reason to smile "   -
Unknown

Day 6

- Look at the list ☐

· Drink 10 glasses ☐

- Complete a DIY ☐

- Do something you have been meaning and procrastinating to do ☐

"Be you,

Do you,

Love you,
For you"

-Unknown

Day 7

· Look at the list ☐

· Meditate ☐

· Do some yoga ☐

· Compliment someone ☐

"You are not required to put yourself on fire to keep others warm "

-Unknown

Day 8

- · Learn a new skill ☐

- · Look at the list ☐

- · Treat yourself (whatever that means to you) ☐

- · · Drink 10 glasses of water ☐

" You alone are enough. You have nothing to prove to anyone " - Maya Angelou

Day 9

- Give back to your community □

- Drink 10 glasses of water □

· Look at the list □

· Make a loved one a list about 30 things □

" When you realize your self- worth, you will stop giving people discounts "

-Unknown

Day 10

· Look at the list ☐

· Reflect on what you have learned about yourself in the last 10 days ☐

· Show a kind act towards yourself ☐

· Give someone a hug ☐

Chapter 9

Happily ever after

I hope that you will apply the teachings and advice from this book into your life. It would be fulfilling to me as the writer to see you to succeed in your quest to find true love. After enduring blistering winds, scorching desserts and high cold mountains to catch a distant glimpse of a sacred tower and approaching it only to be met with a fearless dragon guarding the tower and after slaying the dragon you climb to the top of the highest tower and there it is. A mirror. Your heart suddenly feels calm and you start smiling as you are met with the refection of your true love. The person in the mirror. Suddenly all your wishes are fulfilled, and you are enthralled. You are ready to live your happily ever after.

In all honesty, the Law of Attraction has changed my life for the better, forever and now I can say that I am living a life that I am personally happy with. There are days I walk past the mirror and tell myself how I am so lucky to be me and have the resources I have and there are days where I look in the mirror and cannot help but cry to think that someone would be so mean to such mesmerizing creation and that I, Gloria Azwikonisaho Ramavhuya, would join in and shame me but I am hopeful that if I could get through It then you are my darling fellow creator are no exception. The pain will hurt but it will not break you!

www.ingramcontent.com/pod-product-compliance
Lightning Source LLC
Chambersburg PA
CBHW022345040426
42449CB00006B/724